GEORGIA

Tennessee

North Carolina

VALLEY
AND PLATEAU

Chatahoochee National Forest

Brasstown Bald

APPALACHIAN
MOUNTAINS

Carters Lake

Rome

Lake
Sidney Lanier

Hartwell Lake

N

Alatoonah Lake

Atlanta

Athens

Chatahoochee River

Clarks Hill Lake

PIEDMONT

Augusta

West
Point Lake

Lake Sinclair

Savannah River

Macon

UPPER COASTAL PLAIN

Columbus

South
Carolina

Oconee River

Ogeechee River

Ocmulgee River

Savannah

Altamaha River

Albany

Chattahoochee River

LOWER COASTAL PLAIN

BARRIER ISLANDS AND ESTUARIES

Flint River

Spring River

Satilla
River

Lake Seminole

Valdosta

Okefenokee

Atlantic Ocean

Florida

Swamp

James Randklev

IMAGES OF WILDNESS

GEORGIA

JAMES RANDKLEV

FOREWORD BY DR. EUGENE ODUM

WESTCLIFFE PUBLISHERS, INC. ENGLEWOOD, COLORADO

ACKNOWLEDGEMENTS

Completing this book would have been impossible without the many individuals and organizations who helped research and access unique natural areas. I wish to thank The Nature Conservancy, including Tavia McCuean and Jonathan Streich; The Georgia Conservancy; Georgia Department of Natural Resources, including Harvey Young and Bob Monroe; Freshwater Wetlands and Heritage Inventory Program; Edward J. Noble Foundation; Wassaw Island Trust, including George Quaile; U.S. Department of the Interior; National Park Service; U.S. Fish and Wildlife Service, including John Davis; Georgia State Parks and Historic Sites; Sierra Club, including Steven Johnson; and Fernbank Science Center.

Special recognition and thanks also go to Debbie McIntyre (Little Saint Simons Island), Royce Hayes and Brad Winn (Saint Catherines Island), Mike Broas (Tybee Island), Robert Emery (Panola Mountain State Conservation Park), Paul Tritaik (Bond Swamp National Wildlife Refuge), Tee Brower and Leslie Davenport (Ebenezer Creek), John Pritchett (naturalist), Frankie Snow (South Georgia College), Leon Neel (Tall Timbers), Jonathan Ambrose and Jim Allison (Georgia Department of Natural Resources, Heritage Inventory Program), Frank Manning (Glencoe Taj Airport), and Don Hale (ProLab, Seattle, Washington).

I am most grateful, after a chance meeting on Sosebee Cove Trail, for the assistance of Sharon Worsham, managing editor of this book. The many helpful contacts Sharon provided — as well as the pulling together of information, and caption and commentary writing — are greatly appreciated. Finally, thanks to all the other people who made my journey easier throughout Georgia.

— J.R.

The editors gratefully acknowledge the following scientists for their assistance with captions and commentaries: P.E. Bostick, Kennesaw State College; E. Lloyd Dunn and David B. Dusenbery, Georgia Tech; Robert L. Humphries, U.S. Environmental Protection Agency; Keith Parsons, Thomas S. Patrick and Charles V. Rabolli, Georgia Department of Natural Resources; Jonathan Streich, Georgia Field Office of The Nature Conservancy; Richard G. Wiegert, University of Georgia; and Lawrence A. Wilson, Fernbank Science Center.

— S.W.

Front Cover: Autumn color above Amicalola Falls, Springer Mountain, Amicalola Falls State Park.

First Frontispiece: Native flame azaleas, Callaway Gardens
Second Frontispiece: Ancient oak in tide runnel, South End Beach, Ossabaw Island
Third Frontispiece: Evening primrose, Quitman County
Fourth Frontispiece: Distant Mount Yonah rises above a mixed-hardwood-pine forest, Chattahoochee National Forest
Opposite: Altamaha River flows through Coastal Plain bordered by miles of unspoiled cypress swamp, southeastern Georgia

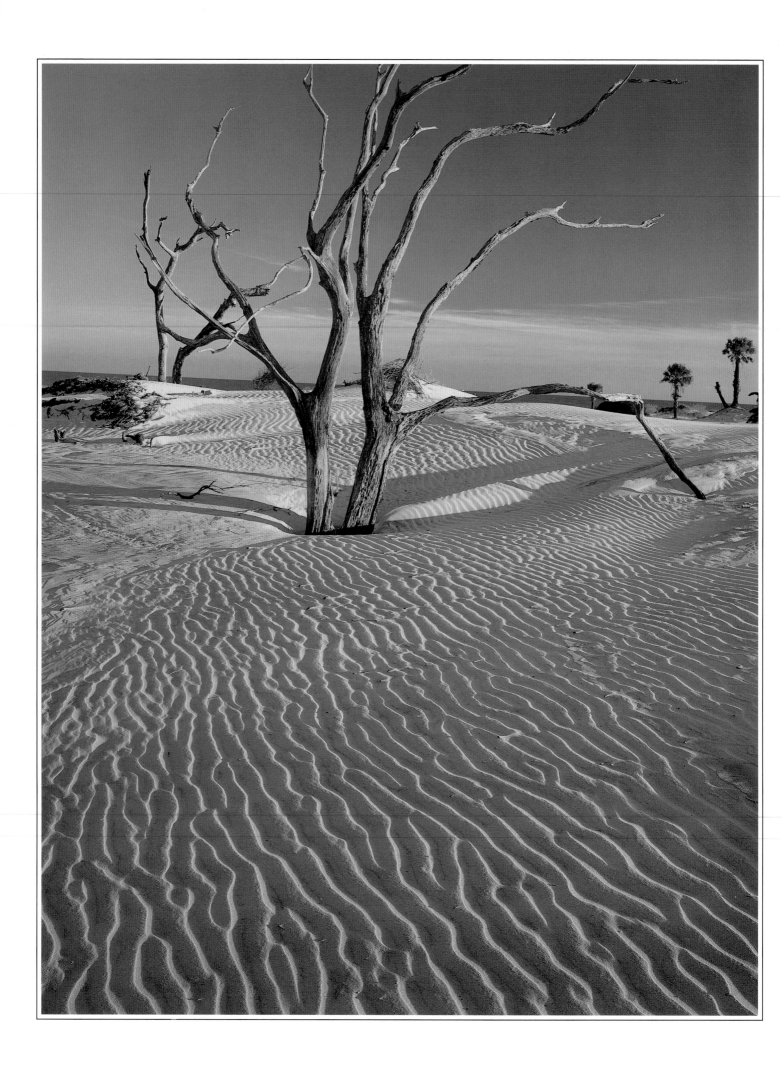

CONTENTS

Opposite: Live oak skeletons, Cumberland Island

Above: White water lilies in Okefenokee Swamp, Stephen Foster State Park

EUGENE P. ODUM

FOREWORD

The Georgia landscape has changed dramatically during the past 50 years. In the 1930s when the Southeast was still in the grips of the Great Depression, all of its old-growth timber had been cut except for pockets of inaccessible swamp forest and stands of virgin longleaf pine on millionaires' plantations in southwestern Georgia. Even most of the virgin cypress in the Okefenokee Swamp had been logged. Native deer and turkey were all but exterminated. Much of the land on the Piedmont, where most Georgians lived then as now, was severely eroded as a result of the world's worst row-crop agriculture. As viewed from its highways, too much of Georgia in those days gave the appearance of a cut-over rural slum.

Today, the landscape in general is much improved. Only the better sites are farmed. Compared with the 1930s, twice the yield of a diversity of agricultural products is obtained from half as much land. Something green — pine trees, grass or cover crops — occupies the abandoned and worn-out cropland, so one sees very little of the red subsoil that once greeted the traveler as either red mud or red dust, depending on the season. Deer and turkeys are everywhere; in fact there are too many deer, about one million, or one deer for every six persons. Soils are being rebuilt and many cut-over forests have regrown.

Various cultural and economic indices indicate that the state as a place for humans to live is now equal to or better than many other states, north or south. Young people who used to leave the state at the first opportunity are now remaining or immigrating in droves.

The land grant state university, a unique American institution, has played a major role in this transformation, affirming the importance of education coupled with agricultural and environmental research. Now a whole new set of challenges must be faced — and soon — since the future of the Georgia environment will be more affected by rapid population growth, urban sprawl, pollution and general affluence than by poverty. Environmental education needs to start in grade school, not be put off until college, so the next generation of decision makers will be much more environmentally literate than is the case now. This is beginning to be undertaken in Georgia, as in other states.

Despite the past abuses of the land and the current demand for development, there are today many wild and scenic areas of exceptional beauty in Georgia, as illustrated by James Randklev's striking photographs. The state's extensive north-south and altitudinal gradient from the mountains to the sea provides a lot of actual and potential biodiversity. Let us hope that this beautiful book can find its way into school libraries. The commentaries introducing each of the state's six physiographic regions, written by some of Georgia's best naturalists and ecologists, make this book an educational treasure.

Two of the state's largest natural areas — the national forests (with small portions designated as wilderness areas) of northern Georgia and the Okefenokee Swamp far to the south — are the locations for many of Randklev's pictures. Both areas were acquired for preservation in the 1930s after most of the valuable old-growth timber had been removed and after an attempt to drain the Okefenokee had failed.

It is fortunate that at about this same time wealthy out-of-state families — the Carnegies, the Rockefellers, the Reynoldses and others — acquired a number of Georgia's sea islands when their real estate value was very low. Ossabaw, one of the largest with 10 miles of beach, was purchased for about $350,000! Falling in love with the islands and wishing to preserve them, the owners were willing to give or sell them cheaply (by today's real estate values) to federal, state or private organizations that would promise to maintain them as natural heritage areas, environmental research parks, wildlife sanctuaries, state parks or national seashores (in the case of Cumberland Island).

A somewhat similar situation exists in the plantation country of southwestern Georgia, where wealthy owners are seeking means to preserve the beauty and utility of their lands. For example, an ecological research center supported by a very large endowment has been established on the Woodruff Plantation in Baker County.

It is also fortunate that following a public outcry over a proposal to strip-mine Georgia's coastal marshes for phosphate — and some good research and educational work at our marine institute on Sapelo Island — the state in 1969 enacted effective legislation to protect the half-million acres of saltmarsh estuaries that lie between the Barrier Islands and the mainland. Because of the high tidal amplitude in the Georgia–South Carolina "bight," these marshes are the most productive and

Opposite: Holly Creek, Cohutta Wilderness

interesting of their kind on the Atlantic seaboard. Continued strong public opinion for preservation and vigilance by conservation agencies are required, because various vested interests are ever ready to propose amendments to the Marsh Protection Act that would allow development to nibble away this magnificent preserve, which provides a buffer between the wildness and recreation values of the islands and the commercial and industrial values of the mainland.

Despite the impressive set-asides at each end of the state, very little natural beauty is protected either by public ownership or private easement in the middle of the state, especially in the vicinity of the nine-county Atlanta hub where more than half of the people of Georgia now live. Statewide, only 8 percent of the area of this very large state is in some kind of protective status. Our goal is to increase this to 20 percent by the year 2000. The opportunity is there, since a great deal of land is on hold, that is, sitting out there waiting for decisions as to how it will be used in the future.

There is reason to be optimistic since recent governors, key legislators and the general public seem to have accepted the 20 percent goal as desirable and doable. But to achieve this goal, greater use will need to be made of conservation easements, bond issues, income tax checkoffs, tax-deduction gifts from large landholders, private conservancy purchases and other means that do not require use of tax money for direct purchase. Additionally, the means to maintain and manage these areas will have to be increased manyfold.

Finally, I want to emphasize that a major reason for preserving lots of natural areas as well as prime farmlands lies in their value in providing vital and mostly non-market life-support goods and services such as clean air, clean water, good soil and so on. Without healthy watersheds, airsheds, wetlands, river corridors, farmlands and the diversity of organisms that contribute to natural recycling and regeneration of these non-market goods and services of nature — cities, industries and other producers of economic wealth cannot prosper.

As land prices rise and shortages develop, people often complain that natural area preservation is an unaffordable luxury because we "can't eat scenery." We can reply by saying, "But we can breathe and drink it, and it can reduce your healthcare costs, maybe even save your life." We can also profit from the enhanced value of private property that lies next to a protected area.

Just recently a team of economists and environmental health scientists published an article in the journal <u>Science</u> that documented in great detail how sickness and death due to bad air in Southern California cost "the economy" billions of dollars each year, not to mention the human misery and crime that also result from a polluted and overcrowded environment.

It should be our God-given right to be able to relieve some of the stress of our increasingly urban life by visiting and enjoying such places of quiet beauty as pictured in James Randklev's photographs without having to take a long trip or spend a lot of money. Unfortunately, our national and international concern for human rights does not as yet include this environmental right, even though it is indirectly guaranteed by our constitution. I'll bet you didn't know or had forgotten that maintaining "domestic tranquility," which we can interpret as "quality of life," is listed along with defense, justice and public welfare as the four responsibilities assigned to the federal government in the preamble of the United States Constitution.

— Eugene P. Odum
Callaway Professor of Ecology Emeritus
and Director Emeritus
Institute of Ecology
University of Georgia, Athens

Opposite: Hickory along Pine Mountain Ridge, Franklin D. Roosevelt State Park

JAMES RANDKLEV

PREFACE

In this place between earth and sky lies a unique landscape known as Georgia. Natural forces have shaped these mountains and valleys, created vast river plains with wetlands and swamps, and given rise to a chain of barrier islands. To the casual visitor, Georgia may seem to be a uniform sea of green undulating across a broken landscape. Instead, it is a region of such diverse contrast that it is difficult to imagine all this wild beauty in one state.

My journey through Georgia began two years ago when I accepted the challenge of photographing its most unique natural areas. However, it was the challenge I wanted: to capture on film all that I could experience.

My first encounter with the Georgia landscape was Cloudland Canyon, which is located in the northwestern corner of the state. I stood motionless on the canyon's rim in disbelief. "Can this be Georgia?" I asked myself. Below me the gorge was a thousand feet deep, cut through sandstone where the west side of Lookout Mountain drops to a valley floor of fossil-bearing limestone. This canyon is home to a rich variety of native hardwoods and countless flowering plants. Spring had not fully developed as I gazed on the textured trunks of bare oak, hickory and gum trees, but already the dogwood and native azalea had unfurled their delicate blossoms.

I had no hesitation in taking the steep trail down to Daniel Creek Falls, for the air was cool and crisp, and the sparkling water danced on the scattered boulders before falling again and again over sandstone ledges. Though the majority of the forest had just begun its springtime renewal, the ground was covered with trilliums, bird's-foot violets and spring-blooming hepaticas. The summit of nearby Pigeon Mountain offered a unique view of oddly shaped sandstone conglomerate boulders, portions of which were striated, honeycombed and weathered by the elements into unusual figures equal to anything found in the rugged western national parks.

This introduction to the Georgia landscape was only a taste of what was to come. My journey that first spring lead me to explore the Appalachians — an ancient mountain range that extends from Georgia to Maine. Though not as dramatic as the western ranges, the Appalachians offer a multitude of hidden treasures for anyone willing to hike their many trails and ridges. The plant life is spectacular, and waterfalls seem to appear as if by magic wherever there is a ravine or watercourse.

Chattahoochee National Forest occupies the majority of the Blue Ridge and Appalachian ranges. Within these boundaries lie pristine environments worthy of classification as wilderness areas, such as the Raven Cliffs Wilderness. At Raven Cliffs I photographed the Fraser magnolia and the sweet birch whose branches carry the strong scent of wintergreen. As I stood in the center of this seemingly impenetrable forest, I felt its peace and imagined that this was what early explorers — Hernando DeSoto in the 16th century and William Bartram in the late 18th century — must also have shared. Unfortunately, there are few environments in Georgia that qualify as wilderness — early European settlers altered this landscape forever.

Georgia's eastern border — shared with South Carolina — is the Chattooga River, designated as a national wild and scenic River in 1974, and often called the crown jewel of southern whitewater rivers. Here I hiked to Bull Sluice Rapid after a heavy spring rain common to the region. I felt the ground trembling from the great force of water funneling through the narrow streambed. The river drops almost 2,000 feet from its headwaters in North Carolina before it reaches Lake Tugalo. Given their relatively small area, the north Georgia mountains offer a wealth of flora and fauna. Subsequent trips brought me a sense of personal renewal and provided some indelible images for this book.

Gazing out across the rocky shoals of the Flint River from Sprewell Bluff, I saw the Piedmont — a broad zone of gently rolling hills situated between the mountains and the coastal plain. Here I found a mixture of biota common to both regions — a delicate blending of pine, mountain laurel, oak and hickory. I discovered floodplain forests of tupelo along the Alcovy. The Palisades on the Chattahoochee River, within the bustling metropolitan area of Atlanta, seemed untouched. I marveled at the old-growth forest adjacent to the Fernbank Science Center, also within Atlanta. This "school in the woods" is the legacy of Miss Emily Harrison, a pioneer conservationist and environmental educator.

Nowhere was I more touched with a sense of wonder than among the granite outcrops of Panola and Stone mountains, and at Heggies Rock. Here I was fascinated with wild dish gardens that showed the genesis of primordial soil formation.

Opposite: Fallen pine cones, wild grapes and native dogwood blanket forest floor, Cumberland Island

Delicate red diamorpha lined the shallow depressions, fringed with crustose lichens and reindeer moss. A multitude of endemic plants, such as the Confederate daisy, grow only upon these islands of granite.

Heading south I arrived at the Upper Coastal Plain where the landscape at first appeared flat, but hidden treasures soon were revealed to me. The colorful limestone-eroded walls of Providence Canyon brought images of whimsical spires reaching skyward. Tupelo swamps, such as the newly protected Bond Swamp, now provide habitats for wood ducks in the hollowed-out trees. The sea once covered this great plain. Receding seas left behind only fossilized remains of shells and plants, as I discovered while hiking the streambed of Town Creek Gorge — a small but enchanting tributary of the Cemochechobee. Unfortunately, a local landfill upstream has made its mark with broken bottles and debris. Hopefully this precious area can be protected for all to enjoy.

In a remote area of Coffee County, my guide, Frankie Snow, lead me through a maze of sandstone outcrops known as Broxton Rocks, exposed long ago from the ancient Ocmulgee River streambed. Here a side stream, Rocky Creek, has created a natural sculpture garden, and its fractured banks are resplendent with ferns, lichens and green-fly orchids. Here we also found more than nature's untrammelled wildness, with litter scattered throughout. It was frustrating to witness such disregard for this unique environment.

The virgin longleaf pine-wiregrass community is something I had heard about for many years. It once covered thousands of square miles of the southeastern United States, but now only small remnants remain. My guide, Leon Neel, took me through the Millpond and Wade plantations where I saw 200-year-old pines, survivors of those cleared by early pioneers while homesteading the pine barrens of southern Georgia. Fire is a vital agent for the renewal of these pine forests, for it prevents plant succession to upland hardwoods. I was also fortunate to find a limestone sinkhole filled with water here — an emerald jewel under the cool October sky.

The Lower Coastal Plain offered a glimpse into the primordial landscapes of blackwater rivers, hardwood hammocks, great river deltas, and a swamp that the Cherokees called Okefenokee, "Land of the Trembling Earth." Born of freshwater springs with islands of ancient peat, the Okefenokee is not a true swamp, but a vast watershed that gives birth to two well-known rivers, the Suwannee and the Saint Marys. Canoeing these tannin-stained waters past water lilies and moss-covered cypress, I felt this was an area relatively untouched by man — until I was told that most of the stands of virgin cypress had been logged a century ago.

Nowhere in Georgia was I more impressed by nature's raw beauty than on the Barrier Islands. Thousands of years ago the Guale Indians hunted and fished these tidal marshes and island retreats along Georgia's coast. At first glance each island appeared the same to me as I flew over a sea of grass dotted with hammocks of hardwoods bordered by windswept beaches. On Cumberland Island I followed well-worn trails among twisted live oaks on a misty morning with only the chatter of palmetto fronds rustling in the sea breeze. I saw distant white dunes covered with golden sea oats and hiked the lonely beach to find countless seashells scattered among the remains of giant horseshoe crabs. These coastal scenes seem unchanged since the dawn of time.

Wassaw Island, with its densely forested interior and freshwater ponds, is the most pristine of the Golden Isles. I hiked the north beach, which boasts a boneyard area of fallen live oaks — abstract sculptures half buried in sand. I felt the brisk salt air stinging my face under November skies with only sanderlings and terns for company.

Ossabaw Island is equally inviting, with its vast tidal marshes where spartina reigns. To watch the ebb and flow of these tidal rivers is to bear witness to the eternal cycle of life.

The Barrier Islands for all their magical beauty have not escaped the hand of man. Native Americans cherished the natural resources and held them in spiritual regard. However, colonizing immigrants established plantations and rapidly depleted those resources for their own interests. Trees fell, swamps were drained and the thin topsoil was soon gone. Fortunately, the isolation and harshness of the elements proved too challenging to man, giving the islands a reprieve from further development, which the mainland was undergoing at that time. With the help of various present-day conservation organizations, the islands may once again return to their natural state, preserved for future generations.

As I drove Georgia's quiet back roads, hiked its many trails and canoed its blackwater rivers and swamps, I realized that the state's greatest resource is her people. In every region I was greeted by friendly folks who care deeply about their beloved state. Through their great love of nature they have spread the word to multitudes by volunteering to clean up natural areas and by teaching others to appreciate Georgia's remaining environmental treasures.

Now is the time to take charge and to protect Georgia's natural heritage and delicate ecosystems — and an individual truly can make a difference. More than 500 acres have been voluntarily registered with the Georgia Natural Areas Registry of The Nature Conservancy by private landowners whose property contains some valuable natural feature, such as the rare relict trillium near the banks of the Cemochechobee Creek or Oglethorpe oak along Buffalo Creek.

Naturalist Henry David Thoreau wrote: "In wildness is the preservation of the world." It is time to cherish this wildness if we are to live in harmony on this planet called Earth.

— JAMES RANDKLEV

Opposite: Springtime at little-known Minnehaha Falls, Rabum County

APPALACHIAN MOUNTAINS

Charles H. Wharton

To climb a high mountain is to travel 1,000 miles north and 20,000 years back into time. In the grip of the last Ice Age, when mastodon and ground sloth lumbered across southern Georgia, the mountains of northern Georgia were much different. Great pine and spruce-fir forests covered the higher mountains with summits of barren alpine tundra, the home of life now found only in Alaska and Canada.

As man hunted and gathered his way southward in post-glacial warmth, a vast hardwood forest crept up the Appalachian slopes, replacing the conifers. The mountaintops became balds, some now shrubby, some rocky, some grassy. Lower talus slopes of rock became boulder fields. Trees such as beech, birch and sugar maple took refuge on the higher, north-facing coves, along with the raven and red squirrel and other relict species left behind with the retreat of the ancient subarctic forests.

Thus, the great eastern deciduous forest biome came into being. The enormous diversity of herbs, shrubs and trees with all their nuts, fruits and leaves supported an abundance of animals. The Cherokee grew to cherish their bountiful and beautiful homeland, but were tragically evicted in 1838.

The settlers who followed found subsistence in tiny cornfields and from nature's larder. These Anglo-Saxon newcomers came to treasure the solitude and peace of their environment. Some cared for Cherokee refugees who hid out in rock shelters. Caucasian man brought change to these wild coves and ridges. The howl of the wolf and the scream of the panther were no longer heard; man became the apex carnivore.

The lure of great swathes of mineral richness — talcs of the Cohuttas, marbles of the Murphy Syncline, gold of the Dahlonega Belt, and corundum, mica and asbestos of the ultramafic zones — helped displace the Cherokee from northern Georgia. The old-growth forests stimulated logging and road building, bringing a new dimension to a simple subsistence way of life, in harmony with the rhythm of nature.

Apart from the valleys, most of the Blue Ridge Province passed to federal stewardship as Chattahoochee National Forest. Now preserved are scenic areas, parks, wilderness and back-country areas, waterfalls, scenic vistas and a few remnants of original forest biodiversity after a century of exploitation.

Old values which regarded a tree chiefly as a source of lumber, are slowly giving way to more realistic visions of sustainability. We now know that the merit of mountain forests rests, not in lumber, but in their value when maintained in a natural state, coupled with ecologically oriented tourism. Another important function of mountain forest is the absorption of waste gases, fallout particles and acid rain, all intensified by human technology.

The environmental importance of the entire bioregion lies in the mountain forests, primarily in the storage and management of water. Beneath the many forest types left behind by the retreating cold, the forest floor is bound by billions of diverse root systems. Over time, layers of leaves and herbs decayed and filled the soil with tiny, water-holding particles of organic matter. Thin soils at high elevations must cope with more than 100 inches of rain annually. The formation and stabilization of an organic-rich soil blanket supports itself and yields pure, surplus water for man's use.

Also addressed is the quality of human life. The north Georgia mountains form an important outdoor classroom. In this refuge from the burgeoning population surrounding it, we may return to an earth-centered consciousness: towering cliffs and rhododendron in bloom, hiking along the seeming rooftop of the world; plunging down a river gorge in a raft or canoe.

Northern Georgia represents the southern terminus of the great Appalachian bioregion. Here, ancient mountains guard the best and wildest displays of life anywhere in the temperate zone. In the mountains we glimpse divine forces that have shaped the ancient bond of man and nature, gaining an understanding of how our own lives can best be perpetuated.

Dr. Charles H. Wharton, living in the north Georgia mountains, holds a position as research associate at The Institute of Ecology. One of Georgia's preeminent naturalists, Wharton wrote The Natural Environments of Georgia *(1977), the only comprehensive volume to date covering Georgia's natural environments. He led in preserving southern wilderness areas and in stopping stream channelization. He was principal consultant for The Georgia Conservancy's* Guidebook to the North Georgia Mountains *and has published extensively on southeastern wetlands.*

Above: Dogwoods and oaks near Neels Gap in early spring, Chattahoochee National Forest
Opposite: Sourwood along the shores of Lake Unicoi, Unicoi State Park

Showy phlox along Panther Creek, Chattahoochee National Forest

Bird's-foot violets, Cohutta Wilderness   Overleaf: Autumn color, from Brasstown Bald — Georgia's highest mountain

Whether observing the pummeling waters of Amicalola Falls, or canoeing the exhilarating whitewater of Amicalola Creek flowing through unspoiled forest below the falls, one's sense of awe and wonder of nature is renewed. Falling for 730 feet, the falls are the highest in Georgia and were aptly named "tumbling waters" by the Cherokee. The surrounding forest is rich with wildflowers, and moist coves are abundant with ferns, mosses and salamanders.

Much of the Georgia mountain environment is characteristic of habitats found farther north, hence this forest meadow of New York ferns (right). Northern species creep down to their southernmost range and many southern species reach their northernmost limits in the Blue Ridge. This contributes to Georgia's ranking by The Nature Conservancy as fifth in the nation in terms of diversity and richness of plant and animal life.

Amicalola Falls, Amicalola Falls State Park

Fallen tree provides nutrients for New York Ferns and spiderworts at Hog Pen Gap, Chattahoochee National Forest

Autumn color at Amicalola Falls, Chattahoochee National Forest

Volunteer day lilies, probably from an old homesite, along Escowee River Falls, Chattahoochee National Forest

A mountain vista brilliant with color is the choice for autumn; a verdant mountain stream dotted with wildflowers is the choice for spring and summer — a demonstration of *periodicity*, the changing seasons. The chief characteristic of a deciduous forest is its display of red carotenes and yellow xanthophylls dominating in fall and green chlorophylls dominating in spring and summer. Intensity of autumn color seems to be due to a combination of summer rain, temperature, soil nutrients and day length. Spring has two color phases: the early pastels with pinks and a multitude of soft yellow-greens followed by the late solid greens, more uniformly dark in color. A winter forest is beautiful in its skeletal nakedness. The only thing constant about nature is change.

White pines in autumn forest of oak, hickory and sweetgum, Nantahala Wilderness

Mountain laurel along Dodd Creek in spring, Raven Cliffs Wilderness

There is incredible beauty in Georgia's winter forest, half naked and half clothed, due to the abundance of both deciduous and evergreen vegetation. Lower stream slopes covered with rhododendron and mountain laurel are always green, even in the face of severe freezing rain that can coat branches with ice and form cascades of frozen waterfalls and icicles. The colder the temperature, the more tightly a rhododendron will curl its leaves like a rolled cigar, probably a protection for reducing water loss through the leaf underparts.

DeSoto Falls Scenic Area is a part of Georgia's vast Chattahoochee National Forest (right). Its name came from the legend that a piece of Hernando DeSoto's armor was found nearby. Dropping a total of more than 300 feet, DeSoto Falls is a picturesque series of four falls spanning five miles of lush mountain terrain.

Icicle-draped rhododendrons, Chattahoochee National Forest

Sheer face of DeSoto Falls with climbing hydrangea, Chattahoochee National Forest

Splendid fall color reflected in its crystalline water, Lake Conasauga is nestled in the interior of the Cohutta Wildlife Management Area at the edge of the Cohutta Wilderness. The Cohutta Wilderness is a vast sweep of lush forest, cascading rivers and streams, and steep ridges at the western edge of Georgia's Blue Ridge Mountains.

Dense forests surrounding lakes and rivers play a significant role in maintaining water purity and clarity. Many of Georgia's major rivers have their headwaters in the Blue Ridge Mountains, including the famous National Wild and Scenic Chattooga River (right). Though scenic to the casual observer, the large boulders, rocky ledges and deep holes contributing to its appeal are deceptively dangerous and sometimes deadly to the unwary or careless whitewater enthusiast — a truly wild river.

Fallen tree in Lake Conasauga, Cohutta Wildlife Management Area

Bull Sluice Rapid, National Wild and Scenic Chattooga River   Overleaf: Tallulah River flows through ravine lined with birch, American hornbeam and tag alder, Chattahoochee National Forest

Native wildflowers abound in this sunny meadow, the result of a disturbed forest. Left to its own recovery plan — undisturbed and in time — the area will revert to pines, then back to a hardwood forest, similar to the one now bordering this meadow.

The mountain beauty of Georgia is seen at magnificent Toccoa Falls (right), an example of a river eroding its way upstream through hard bedrock. Unlike the young water-absorbing sedimentary sandstone of the plateau region, the hard metamorphic rock of the Blue Ridge sheds water — one reason for the abundance of waterfalls found in the north Georgia mountains. These streams support many native species, including the brook trout and a large salamander, the hellbender, which has been known to reach 30 inches in length. Preserving the natural character of the mountain region as a watershed resource and for recreation and education is most important.

Black-eyed Susans and daisy fleabanes blanket meadow at Warwoman Dell, Rabun County

Rainbow at Toccoa Falls, Toccoa

VALLEY AND PLATEAU

Philip Greear

To the interstate highway traveler, northwestern Georgia's images of wildness are infinitesimally fleet. To the back-road blue-highway rider they are fleet, but perceptible. To the foot traveller the images of wildness are experienced in intimate detail. We see the valued remnants of millions of years of natural history.

The Appalachian region in Georgia is delineated by the Smoky Mountain–Cartersville Fault. East and south of this fault system lie the Blue Ridge and Piedmont provinces made up of ancient crystalline or igneous rocks, while the Valley and Ridge and the Cumberland Plateau rocks consist entirely of sedimentary materials.

Tectonic forces have caused the sedimentary materials to be folded up and down, thrusting older sediments over younger rocks. Constant erosion has taken place throughout millions of years. Since some rocks are harder than others, the alternating ridge and valley topography has developed.

The region is made up of two prominent land forms: the Cumberland Plateau and the Valley and Ridge Provinces. The Cumberland Plateau is represented by several flat-topped, mesa-like narrow ridges such as Sand Mountain, Lookout Mountain (100 miles long with 21 miles in Georgia and extending 3 miles into Tennessee and 76 miles into Alabama), Little Sand Mountain and Rock Mountain. Among the prominent ridges, the most spectacular is Taylor's Ridge, extending from south of Summerville well into Tennessee. Others are Johns, Lavender, Sims and Horseleg mountains. Between these rises are lush pastoral valleys, some of which are 10 to 20 miles wide while others measure less than one mile.

As is true in most of the temperate world, geophysical features dictate the way people use land. The wildness that remains in northwestern Georgia is due to unused landforms.

In the Appalachian region rain falls equally — about 50 inches per year — on both the south- and north-facing slopes. However, sunshine on the south-facing slopes dries things out so rapidly that xeric plants — those adapted to dry conditions — thrive here. The less sunny north-facing slopes nourish plants that require more moisture. Oak, maple and beech are found here in great number. In the fall, the north-facing slopes are more spectacular than others because these moisture-loving

mesic deciduous trees dominate.

Unique natural environments are scattered throughout the Appalachian plateaus and ridges. Lookout Mountain is a synclinal plateau that forms a trough of very hard, pebble-bearing sandstone. Sitton Gulch in Cloudland Canyon State Park is accessible by a trail from which hikers can see remnant communities of the medium-moisture-loving mixed mesophytic trees, shrubs and herbs. Rimrock on Lookout and Pigeon mountains has eroded differentially, leaving intriguing rock castle formations which provide habitat for plants adapted to limited water supply.

The valleys between the ridges are modified by agricultural and urban use. In any valley, Virginia juniper (red cedar) grows profusely in protected places; a calcium-loving tree, wherever it grows in great numbers there is limestone nearby. When the limestone is really shallow, holding water well, a cedar glade forms. There is only one true cedar glade in Georgia, and it has been protected because it occurs within the boundaries of the Chickamauga National Military Park.

Every valley has a creek or river, and the wild communities of plants and animals are found along their banks. These streams are best viewed from a canoe, and all of these streams are navigable by canoe.

There are too many special ecosystems in this diverse region to name them all, but I would be negligent not to mention the sag ponds in Bartow County. Similar to the limesinks of southern Georgia, these are natural depressions around which I have found 23 species of plants which had previously been found only on the Coastal Plain.

Dr. Philip Greear, retired professor and chairman of the Biology and Earth Sciences Division at Shorter College, has been called God's gift to natural causes. He has fought and won many ecological battles and won numerous awards for his advocacy efforts and for contributions to environmental education, including the prestigious National Silver Medal Award from Federated Garden Clubs of America. He is currently working on a state-sponsored coastal ecology education program for middle schoolers. Greear coined the term sag pond ecology. He is a trustee for The Nature Conservancy.

Above: Sunset over the Cumberland Plateau, from Johns Mountain
Opposite: Autumn sunset at Cloudland Canyon, Cloudland Canyon State Park

Split rock in cedar glade, Chickamauga National Military Park

Stalwart red maple at Lookout Lake, Cumberland Plateau

Rock Town is a fascinating jumble of fractured fossil sandstone. Millions of years of weathering of its horizontal planes and vertical joints have resulted in a maze of crevices, ledges, tunnels and bizarre formations. It is an undisturbed and protected natural area that is part of the 13,000-acre Crockford–Pigeon Mountain Wildlife Management Area near La Fayette and stretches for 10 miles southwest to Lookout Mountain. Pigeon Mountain was named for the now-extinct passenger pigeon that roosted here by the thousands during fall migrations in the 1800s.

The deeply eroded rock formations of the Cumberland Plateau support great diversity. The upper rock surfaces are extremely dry with vegetation that is drought-resistant. The lower levels are cool and moist, supporting moisture-loving plants. The cool, refreshing surroundings of Daniel Creek in Cloudland Canyon (right) are a good example of these lower reaches of the Cumberland Plateau.

Lichen-covered sandstone blocks at Rock Town, Pigeon Mountain

Autumn reflections at upper Daniel Creek, Cloudland Canyon State Park

This wonderful old shortleaf pine may have been present when the first Europeans settled the area around 1832, because Marshall Forest has never been logged (above). The presence of a few large pines among younger hardwoods usually indicates that a forest has been cut. However, in Marshall Forest its presence is thought to be due to natural catastrophe. A walk in these woods is like going back hundreds of years in time.

With its extensive vistas and deep ravines — one of the most scenic parks in the state — Cloudland Canyon State Park straddles a deep gorge cut into Lookout Mountain by Sitton Gulch Creek (right). The gorge is considered a reentrant valley. The creek formerly flowed across the top of this ancient tableland, but eventually eroded the sandstone layer at its streamhead as it cut about two miles into the mountain, creating Sitton Gulch.

Mature shortleaf pine among young hardwoods in Marshall Forest, a preserve of The Nature Conservancy

Autumn color at Sitton Gulch, Cloudland Canyon State Park

This 250-acre preserve within the city limits of Rome, Georgia is a remnant jewel in our rapidly diminishing store of natural treasures. Marshall Forest is the only near-original forest community remaining in the Valley and Ridge Province and became Georgia's first national natural landmark in 1966. An extremely diverse old-growth forest, it is home to a great profusion of trees, shrubs, vines, herbs and wildflowers.

Abstracted beauty of form and shape abound in the eroded sandstone of the Cumberland Plateau. At Rock Town the differential erosion of hard and soft rock is the result of millions of years of water seepage through sedimentary materials (right). The subtle yellow-orange colors indicate the presence of iron oxide. Rock Town was once the bottom of an ancient shallow sea. When the seas receded, a network of cracks and holes formed; subsequent deposition and erosion produced the interesting shapes and markings.

Hawk wing remains on oak root in Marshall Forest, a preserve of The Nature Conservancy

Sassafras sprigs at Rock Town, Pigeon Mountain

PIEDMONT

Harvey L. Ragsdale

In Georgia, the Piedmont region tilts north to south from the northern foothills to an abrupt juncture with the Coastal Plain. The hilly northern portion of the Piedmont ranges from 1000 to 2000 feet of elevation with hills of 300 to 600 feet in relief. Moving south to the central Piedmont, the general elevation falls to about 1000 feet on a gently rolling terrain where the hills are 100 to 200 feet high. Continuing south, elevation smoothly declines to about 500 feet with hills of 50 to 100 feet.

The southern terminus of the Piedmont ends abruptly at the fall line, a dramatic change of elevation which creates waterfalls in streams flowing from the Piedmont into the Upper Coastal Plain. This geomorphic feature is culturally significant, since historically these waterfalls provided power for manufacturing and represented the headwaters for transportation waterways.

The forests of the Piedmont fall within a region called oak-pine forest, but this fails to convey their enormous diversity. In maturing Piedmont forests, large pines, shortleaf pines and the ubiquitous loblolly pines grow over 100 feet tall, contributing to a distinctive canopy of evergreen and deciduous tree crowns. Mature forest is rare, but oak, hickory and the towering tulip poplar are the characteristic canopy species.

The history of the land of the Piedmont is one of continual and substantial disruption from agriculture, forestry and urban development. Land abuse from cotton farming eroded topsoils over a 100-year period, ending in 1930. Disruptive cultural activity has produced a mosaic of forests and forest revegetation stages on the Piedmont landscape. This mosaic includes early revegetation characterized by herbs and shrubs; early forest stages dominated by young loblolly pines; later forest stages which have greater numbers of deciduous trees.

The hilly topography of the northern Piedmont provides a variety of micro-habitats, increasing the forest diversity. North-facing slopes are cooler and support more northern species such as white pine, eastern hemlock, beech, red ash, and several deciduous magnolias. The evergreen southern magnolia is abundant near the fall line but is scarce in the northern Piedmont, the geographic extent of its occurrence.

Deep ravines and escarpments along rivers also support development of more northern species. The warmer and drier

south-facing slopes may support a variety of pines, including pitch pine which characteristically occurs in the southern Appalachians. A similar phenomenon occurs in the southern Piedmont where Coastal Plain species migrate into the southern Piedmont region. The Piedmont, therefore, has its characteristic species as well as species from the north and the south. Culturally driven land use, climate, micro-habitats and geographic proximity to other regions enhance natural diversity, spreading over the landscape like a patchwork quilt.

Precambrian metamorphic rocks, formed more than 570 million years ago, underlie the Piedmont soils. Some granite rocks have been exposed by centuries of erosion and now extend over areas known as granite outcrops. Stone Mountain, a granite monadnock near Atlanta, is famous because of its size and elevation over other summits of the Piedmont. There are other smaller elevated outcrops and many flat expanses of granite surrounded by forest. They all share distinctive vegetation, which includes several species endemic only to the outcrops.

The weathered surface of the granite outcrop is covered with an array of lichens that color the surface and whose color changes depending on moisture content. Drainage over the rock becomes channeled, providing enough moisture to support a black rock moss. Depressions of a few centimeters to a meter or more allow sand, rock and organic fragments to accumulate. These depressions can support a variety of annual and perennial plants whose flowering cycles bring brilliant colors to the grey-green surface. The most famous of these perennials is the Confederate daisy whose colorful flowering is formally celebrated each year at Stone Mountain.

Dr. Harvey L. Ragsdale is professor of biology and director of the Human and Natural Ecology Program at Emory University. He has done ecological research in recent years concerning air pollution and acid rain, trace metals in forest watersheds and various aspects of forest decline. As an involved citizen, Ragsdale speaks to numerous local groups about the environment, has served on various environmental advisory committees, and is a trustee for Fernbank, Inc. He has served as consultant for a number of ecological projects.

Above: Azalea blossoms, Callaway Gardens   Opposite: Rhododendrons and mountain laurel, Callaway Gardens

The unique desert-like granite outcrops of the Piedmont are a dramatic contrast to the ever-wet shoals of its many creeks and streams. An exposed granite outcrop is an example of primary succession. Barren rock becomes encrusted with lichens that grow as little as one inch in 60 years. Lichens assist in erosion of rock and help to trap windblown grit and plant debris in crevices and depressions to form soils which then support the growth of larger plants. These special ecosystems support several state and federally protected plants including quillworts, stonecrop and pool sprite, as well as the showy September-blooming Confederate daisy (above), a wildflower that is native to and found only on Georgia's granite outcrops.

Native and rare wildflowers also bloom along Flat Shoals Creek (right), a Piedmont fall line stream. Owned by the same family for 160 years, it has remained relatively undisturbed and unpolluted.

Lichen-encrusted granite outcrop with Confederate daisies on Panola Mountain,
Panola Mountain State Conservation Park

Native sweet azaleas at flooding Flat Shoals Creek, a registered natural area with The Nature Conservancy

Dish gardens of red sedum in spring at Heggies Rock, a preserve of The Nature Conservancy

Wind and water are two of nature's most prolific sculptors, carving out their art on the Piedmont's generous supply of exposed granite — whether on a rocky creekbed of one of the region's few remaining pristine waterways, the Alcovy River (above), or on a primal granite outcrop designated a national natural landmark such as Heggies Rock (left).

Granite outcrop weathering pits become beautiful miniature dish gardens if left undisturbed. They harbor a bright red endemic flowering succulent, the diamorpha or red sedum, which begins growing in late fall rains, bursts into white bloom in spring, and dies back in the summer heat. These succulents store water in their leaves and can grow in as little as one inch of soil. Fairy shrimp and aquatic roly-poly isopods are sometimes found in the temporary pools of these weathering pits. They survive by laying drought-resistant eggs which hatch when wet.

Water-sculpted pools, along the Alcovy River

English ivy on mature hardwoods of a 65-acre relict urban forest, Fernbank Forest,
Fernbank Science Center, metropolitan Atlanta

Hairy-cap moss and pine seedlings in granite weathering pit, Panola Mountain State Conservation Park
Overleaf: Native flame azaleas and bracken ferns, Callaway Gardens

The Flint River (above) begins coursing its way through the Piedmont just south of Atlanta, merging with the Chattahoochee at the Florida border. Since many plants and animals of the Coastal Plain migrate upstream into the Piedmont, these are unique river systems where an unusual blending of Coastal Plain and Piedmont species occur. The endemic Barbour's map turtle with its intricately patterned shell and the alligator snapping turtle are Flint River residents.

The Chattahoochee River (right) begins its journey to the Gulf as a small stream in the Georgia mountains. As it passes through Atlanta it is still wild and most scenic. It winds its way through a variety of landscapes, including islands and rocky shoals, interspersed by calmer waters. At some points, massive granite palisades overhung with rhododendron and mountain laurel rise above the river. Remaining cold enough for trout as far south as Atlanta, it is common to see fly-fishermen wading and casting into the icy waters.

The upper reaches of the Flint River, from Sprewell Bluff

Boulders in the Chattahoochee River as it flows through metropolitan Atlanta,
Chattahoochee River National Recreation Area

Waters of Factory Shoals at Sweetwater Creek, Sweetwater Creek State Conservation Park

This moss-lichen dish garden at Heggies Rock typifies secondary stage plant succession with its reindeer moss lichens, hairy spike moss and spiderwort. Described as the most outstanding national natural landmark in the eastern United States, Heggies Rock is a 100-acre exposed granite outcrop preserve of The Nature Conservancy. Eleven of the 19 plants known only to granite outcrops, as well as 21 other characteristic species, occur at this site.

In contrast to the dry flat-rock outcrop, splashing, pummeling Factory Shoals at Sweetwater Creek State Conservation Park (left) is typical of a Piedmont stream with areas of rapid rock-ledge drops coupled with stretches of meandering flat water. The 30-foot drop just below these shoals is a favorite run of whitewater canoeists during spring floods. During the 1800s many of the rapid drops were utilized to power cotton textile mills, and their ruins can be found along numerous streams of the Piedmont.

Spiderweb on spiderwort, reindeer moss and twisted-hair spike moss at Heggies Rock, a preserve of The Nature Conservancy

Fading light on loblolly pine on South Fork of the Broad River, Watson Mill Bridge State Park

Loblolly pines on Stone Mountain, Stone Mountain Park

UPPER COASTAL PLAIN

Milton N. Hopkins

Shallow seas once covered the Upper Coastal Plain. Evidence of ancient marine life abounds. The old sea bottom, a relatively flat landscape, covers almost one-third of the state. Upland were the mile after mile of park-like longleaf pinelands carpeted by wiregrass. Most of the virgin pine was gone by 1900. The good soils of the Upper Coastal Plain are the breadbasket of the state.

After 40 years on the farm and out-of-doors, I found it agonizingly impossible to describe the area on one page. I decided on five favorite habitats that are diverse and special. To the southwest, the Dougherty Plain is an unusual area which has many often steep-sided sloped depressions, locally called limesinks. Blue springs abound along rivers where major streams have cut into the limestone aquifer which supplies almost 50 percent of Georgia's ground water.

Special to Georgia's Coastal Plain are some expansive sandstone outcrops. The best example is Broxton Rocks, lying in the central upper plain in Coffee County. Deep erosional crevices bisect hills overlooking Rocky Creek. Disjunct populations of more northern plants occur here, as does the rare Georgia plume. Green-fly orchids cling to dripping sandstone walls, and scarce dwarf filmy ferns grow in moist crevices. On adjacent uplands, nighthawks find nesting sites among lichen-covered rocks and sparse vegetation. In contrast, dead-end caves serve as ideally secluded nesting sites for vultures, birds that have long incubation and fledgling periods.

The Big Bend section of the Ocmulgee River remains relatively unspoiled. Imposing 50-foot bluffs rise above the river and face an expansive floodplain northward. Crystal-clear springs are abundant with needle fish, mullet, shad, striped bass and sturgeon. Mississippi and swallow-tailed kites cruise the skies above river and floodplain forest and find nesting sites here. In groups of 12 to 15, swallow-tails with 50-inch wingspreads spiral from treetop level to 1,500 feet, on thermals.

Carolina Bays are distinctive egg-shaped wetland ecosystems of uncertain origin with an incredible variety of biotic communities and provide protective places for nesting birds. Big Duke's Pond in the eastern uplands is an important Carolina Bay ringed by a narrow marsh zone. Pond cypress dominate in deeper water. As is characteristic of the bays, a raised-rim

sand ridge borders its southeastern quadrant. Georgia's most successful colony of the endangered wood stork is found here. Other fauna are timber rattlers and cottonmouth moccasins. Alligators serve as protectors of wading bird colonies in that they keep four-footed predators, especially raccoons, from swimming out and climbing the nest trees. The sound of bull 'gators roaring adds to the sense of wildness.

Loblolly pines line Seventeen Mile Creek. Titi shrubs grow tree-size near the sand ridge of this ecologically significant creek. Barred owls call, and pileated woodpeckers rap on hollow trees. Thousands of spider lily blossoms and goldenclub line the stream bank. Here, old-timers know about the redhorse sucker runs during the first full moon in April. On the east side of the creek, sandhills cover vast areas and support the gopher tortoise and the endangered indigo snake.

Nowhere else in the Coastal Plain is found such variety and beauty in wildflowers than in the highly acidic pitcher plant bogs. A pineland site in Ben Hill County has yellow, hooded and parrot pitcher plants, sundews, lilies, marsh pinks, hatpins, hardheads, star grass and orchids. Bogs are also home to bog crayfish, earthworms and pitcher plant mosquitoes. Bachman sparrows make conical ground nests on the outer, drier bog fringes. Frequent natural fires seem to augment the growth and preservation of these interesting bogs.

Armadillos and coyotes are now a common sight on the farm. Neither animal seems to have any bad habits. Historically, introductions of non-native animals into new habitats result in the usurpation of native species.

Milton N. Hopkins considers himself a "happy dirt farmer and bird watcher." His farm is in Irwin County. One of Georgia's most knowledgeable naturalists, he holds zoology and ecology degrees from the University of Georgia. He discovered a rare nesting site for wood storks, has a fish named after him, has banded hundreds of birds, authored The Birdlife of Ben Hill County, *has collected specimens for scientific institutions, and was named Soil and Water Conservationist of the Year in 1973 and 1980. He joined the Georgia Ornithological Society at age 12 and has been studying birds for more than 50 years.*

Above: Oak leaves caught on palm ferns and liverworts, Cemochechobee Creek Gorge
Opposite: Pond cypress in autumn, George L. Smith II State Park

Fallen wisteria blossoms among oak leaves and pine cones, Providence Canyon State Conservation Park

Cultivated red clover and purple vetch provide roadside stabilization, Coffee County

Cypress, tupelo and sweetgum along tannin-stained Ogeechee River

Wiry immature longleaf pine seedlings are fondly referred to as "bottlebrushes." Their long moist needles provide protection against fires, whereas mid-size pines are vulnerable to ground fires caused by lightning. The bottlebrush seedlings remain immature for about 10 years, concentrating energy into developing a large root system that will allow them to grow rapidly through the vulnerable mid-size stage. Once mature, they can survive fires that burn the thick grasses below. These bottlebrushes are known as trees with "more root than shoot."

Both the open longleaf pine forest and the slow-moving, mysterious blackwaters of the Ogeechee River (left) are characteristic communities of the Upper Coastal Plain. Surprisingly clean, the river's tea-colored water is the result of tannins produced by plant leaves that drop into the water, decompose and release their tannic acid.

Longleaf pine seedlings among the grasses after a natural burn, Wade Plantation
Overleaf: Skeletal remains of trees rise from small pond, near Lake Seminole

There are few natural lakes in Georgia. Lake Seminole, a picturesque and tranquil place to bird-watch and fish, is a water impoundment forming a large reservoir on the Florida border. Before impoundment, this area surrounded the convergence of Spring Creek and the Flint River with the Chattahoochee, forming the Apalachicola River in Florida. Impoundments change the character of an area. Increased amounts of standing water provide for excellent bird rookeries and as well as mosquito breeding grounds. Often there are increased numbers of sport fish such as largemouth and striped bass, but the exclusion of many native fish may also occur.

Flowing into Lake Seminole, Spring Creek is one of the loveliest streams in the state, with white sand shallows, periodic rocky shoals and picturesque limestone bluffs draped with moss and ferns. The entrance to Godby Springs (right), one of the boils that feed Spring Creek, has a solid limestone bottom interestingly pitted by erosion, visible through its clear blue-green water.

Sunset over Lake Seminole, Seminole State Park

Crystal-clear waters at Godby Springs, Spring Creek

Cypress trunks rise from the Altamaha River swamp, Big Hammock Natural Area

Braided stream in canyon bottom, Providence Canyon State Conservation Park

A wetland wilderness only seven miles from the city of Macon, Bond Swamp National Wildlife Refuge along the Ocmulgee River is an ecologically unique area. It is home to a multitude of waterfowl and wading birds, deer, turkey, beaver, alligator and even black bear. It contains one of the few stretches of undisturbed forested wetlands left in the Southeast. Its dominant tree is the water tupelo, with its sturdy buttressed base that gives support in soft swamp soil.

A scenic wonderland, Broxton Rocks with its boulder fields, ledges and ravines, crevices and waterfalls, comprises an expansive outcrop of ancient sandstone formations (right). It is described as the best example of this type of outcrop in the Georgia Coastal Plain, harboring many rare plants in need of protection. Normally found growing on trees, the rare green-fly orchid miraculously flourishes on the rocks and in shady ravine crevices.

Water tupelo, Bond Swamp National Wildlife Refuge

Sandstone outcrop with resurrection fern, green-fly orchid and numerous oak species, Broxton Rocks

Providence Canyon, Providence Canyon State Conservation Park

Junglelike in its luxuriant and exotic vegetation, the remote Alapaha River winds through a swampy wonderland teeming with wildlife. One of Georgia's protected wild rivers, its upper reaches follow a course of loops and tight turns, shoals and small drops caused by the underlying strata of limestone. Downstream it broadens out with white sand bars and an occasional sandbank bluff up to 10 feet high. Streams like this support river otter, beavers, numerous turtles and snakes, many wading birds, herons and ibis, and slow-swimming fish such as bowfins and gars.

Although known for its breathtaking colors and western look of exposed soil layers, Providence Canyon (left) did not occur naturally. Rather, it is the result of poor farming practices which caused massive erosion. A great number of wildflowers bloom around the canyon rim area in midsummer, including the threatened brilliant red-orange plumleaf azalea.

Loblolly pine, upper reaches of the Alapaha River

Introduced freshwater clams have proven invasive, wiping out many native mollusks, Ohoopee River

Tupelo and water oak leaves on reindeer moss, Kolomoki Creek Gorge

Large limesinks occur naturally in regions underlain with limestone. Water erodes underground caverns which eventually collapse. Some limesinks hold water; others remain dry. The majority have fluctuating water levels. These periodic waters are void of fish, except for an occasional mosquitofish brought in on a bird's feet. However, limesinks are excellent breeding places for amphibians such as frogs, salamanders and newts since many fill with water in spring and have no predator fish.

Buried in the blue marl of Town Creek Gorge (right) are nearly 30 million years of fossilized leaves, oyster reefs and corals, evidence of an ancient sea that rose and fell over time, leaving this imprint. The bluish-clay gorge walls are almost vertical and more than 100 feet deep in places. Ferns are prolific and 300-year-old laurel oaks line the rim. The rare relict trillium, found in only six places in the world, grows nearby on private, protected land.

Limestone sinkhole, Millpond Plantation

Ferns and liverworts on blue marl walls of Town Creek Gorge, a tributary of Cemochechobee Creek

Bubbling up from below ledges of weathered limestone and preserved cypress logs, Godby Springs generates a shallow surface stream that drains into nearby Spring Creek. These streamlets and springs are like thin, polished glass, providing a perfect view of their underwater wonderlands. The cypress knees surrounding Godby Springs are thought to supply oxygen to the submerged cypress roots.

The Ohoopee Dunes (right), created by ancient wind action, are Georgia's prehistoric desert. Officially discovered only two decades ago via satellite photographs, these ancient sand dunes were spotted primarily because of their markedly scaled-down vegetation. One small twisted sand oak six inches in diameter was reported to be 138 years old. Stretching along the east banks of the Ohoopee and Canoochee Rivers for 35 miles, these sandhills are a miniature fairyland of lichens and mosses, dwarfed oaks, rare and aromatic mints and rosemary. The dunes are also home to numerous threatened or endangered animals: the indigo snake, gopher tortoise and red-cockaded woodpecker.

Cypress knees and fallen branchlets at rim of Godby Springs, Spring Creek

Reindeer moss, rosemary and live oaks, Ohoopee Dunes

LOWER COASTAL PLAIN

Robert L. Humphries

Georgia's lower Coastal Plain — the pine flatwoods to some — is composed of a series of ancient marine terraces and associated barrier islands formed during repeated incursions of the sea from the late Miocene epoch, about 5 million years ago, to the present. During formation these terraces would have looked much like today's coast with salt marsh behind and barrier island seaward. Of course, in the intervening time, erosion and other processes have brought about changes and created many natural features.

Perhaps the most notable feature of the Lower Coastal Plain is the Okefenokee Swamp, a 681-square-mile, near-wilderness of cypress and/or tupelo forests, watery prairies of water lilies, spatterdock and goldenclub, 'gators and cottonmouths.

The swamp was once a lagoon of the ocean set off by a natural barrier bar ridge. As the seas receded, the depression and ridge remained, and the area became freshwater swamp. Continued peat formation is filling in the basin, so that the Okefenokee is gradually becoming upland. Wildfires once burned away the peat, keeping the swamp in existence. In a misguided effort, man built a low dam on the Suwannee River to keep more water in the swamp. This prevented natural fires and is thus accelerating the upland-building process.

The swamp is the headwaters for both the Saint Marys and Suwannee rivers. In the 1800s an abortive attempt was made to drain the swamp by digging a canal to the lower Saint Marys. Today the canal remnant provides access to the swamp from the east at Camp Cornelia. The other primary access is through the "Pocket" and Billy's Lake near Fargo on the west.

Reminiscent of the Okefenokee are beautiful Banks Lake/Grand Bay near Lakeland — several thousand acres of open water as well as thousands of acres of cypress-tupelo swamp. It is also Georgia's best example of Carolina Bays — oval depressions which some believe to be scars of ancient meteorite impacts. The area is made up of several overlapping bays, readily seen on aerial photographs. Part of the area is a wildlife management area and a popular recreation spot.

Rivers that arise on the Coastal Plain are often called blackwater rivers. Tea-colored by the decaying organic matter in adjacent swamps, the water is still transparent. Rivers such as

the Satilla, Alapaha and Ohoopee are striking, with their dark water contrasting against the white sand bars in the river bends.

Associated with several of the rivers of the Lower Coastal Plain are large, deep arc-shaped, pure white sand dunes. These extremely dry areas are always on the eastern side of a stream and are thought to be wind deposits from the Pleistocene epoch about 2 million years ago. They present a unique appearance with the very dark-leaved dwarf live oak and the British Soldier lichens. Blooming in July, the particularly rare Georgia plume may be found at these sites. The Big Hammock Natural Area may be a small example of arc-shaped dunes associated with the Altamaha River. The most well-known examples are the Ohoopee Dunes where Interstate 16 crosses the Altamaha River.

Another aspect is presented near the mouth of Ebenezer Creek. This easily canoed creek runs in a broad floodplain of the Savannah River valley, with water levels that may vary six to eight feet. Here one will find cypress and tupelo with large buttressed bases — as much as 12 feet in diameter. The tupelo are notable because their trunks twist counterclockwise.

The larger rivers which flow through the Coastal Plain from the upland — the Savannah and the Altamaha — form large estuarine freshwater swamps when they encounter Georgia's extremely high tides. It is in this area that rice culture flourished during slavery times. Two areas remain in these swamps where virgin cypress, tupelo, ash and black gum can still be found, thanks to inaccessibility: Bear Island on the Savannah River and Lewis Island on the Altamaha River.

Robert L. Humphries, life scientist with the Environmental Protection Agency in Atlanta, formerly director of EPA Office of Congressional and External Affairs, and a zoologist from the University of Georgia, thinks of himself as an "old time naturalist." When not behind his desk, he may be found tramping about the Coastal Plain, He co-discovered, with Milton Hopkins, Georgia's rare wood stork nesting site. As a spokesman for EPA, Humphries has dealt with issues as diverse as hazardous waste control, air and water pollution and radiation.

Above: Hooded pitcher plants in pitcher plant bog, Lower Coastal Plain
Opposite: Evening light on cypress in the "Land of the Trembling Earth," Okefenokee Swamp

White water lilies in the Pocket area, Okefenokee Swamp

Marshland laced with tidal creeks and rivers, Lower Coastal Plain merging with the Barrier Islands
Overleaf: Moss-draped cypress at sunset, Banks Lake National Wildlife Refuge

A blended palette from shades of indigo to tints of sky blue reflect in the deep blackwaters of the serene Satilla River. The deeper waters of these Georgia Coastal Plain blackwater rivers appear black, but when shallow (opposite page), the waters appear tea-colored, stained by the tannic acid of decaying vegetation in upstream swamps.

The Satilla winds its way through a floodplain forest of swamp tupelo with scattered cypress. Its sandy banks, sometimes eight feet high, support a luxurious undergrowth including titi and a native azalea that sets the riverbanks aflame with color in early spring. On its journey to the Atlantic through 12 counties, the Satilla forms the largest blackwater river system — including its tributary streams — situated entirely within the state of Georgia.

Sand terraces along unspoiled blackwater stream, Satilla River

Blackwater streams of burnished-copper water over bright-white sand, such as the lower Alapaha, are fascinating. Along the river one is presented periodically with the stunning contrast of a deep black pool nuzzled against the bright white of an exposed sand bar. These streams are not only beautiful, they are also culturally valuable, recharging the water table during prolonged flood periods and degrading pollution as it is dispersed over large wetland areas.

The flora and fauna of blackwater river systems are adapted to their drastically fluctuating water levels — from winter-spring floods that inundate for long periods of time to dry periods in the autumn. Though oxygen-poor and highly acidic, their waters are host to many tiny insect larvae which support a food chain that includes largemouth bass, water snakes, cotton-mouths, turtles and alligators.

Tea-colored waters above white sand bar, Lower Alapaha River

Suwannee Canal and white water lilies, Okefenokee Swamp

Sunlight filters through the river's canopy. A heavy stillness hangs over the swamp. The vast Okefenokee Swamp and the blackwater Withlacoochee River, each distinctively beautiful, illustrate two of the varied wetland types of the Lower Coastal Plain. Intimate, shaded and scenic, the lower Withlacoochee passes quietly into Florida, flowing into the Suwannee River that drains the Okefenokee.

In contrast to a blackwater river corridor, the great Okefenokee Swamp is a vast saucer-shaped peat bog filling a huge sandy depression which was once part of an ancient ocean floor. It provided a protected and stable environment where myriads of flora and fauna developed and flourished. Today, it is a national wildlife refuge and wilderness area containing several types of habitat — including vegetation-choked watercourses and lakes, open prairies, cypress bogs, sphagnum peat bogs, forested hardwood hammocks and pine barrens.

Red maples and tupelo mirrored in blackwater, lower Withlacoochee River

White water lilies and goldenclub with cypress in the Suwannee Canal, Okefenokee Swamp

The magic of the Okefenokee (left) was as alive for the Indians who lived there centuries ago and named it "Land of the Trembling Earth" as it is for us today. To canoe its watercourses or to step onto a floating island of peat — which shakes underfoot but supports a forest of trees — is to understand its name. Shallow, dark waters of the Okefenokee flow slowly but continuously across the swamp to feed two great rivers: the famed Suwannee (above) on its southwestern border and the historic Saint Marys to the southeast.

  The Okefenokee is America's largest wooded swamp, but to remain a swamp it is dependent upon periodic fires. Occasional severe fires during natural periods of drought burn deep into the peat, creating open bogs and prairies. These swamp habitats may eventually fill in, becoming forested hammocks unless fires are allowed as an integral part of the ecosystem.

Blackwater reflections on Suwannee River, Okefenokee Swamp

Here on the Lower Coastal Plain, broad floodplain swamps (above) and slow-moving sinuous rivers (right) give us a sense of going back in geologic time to the primeval swamplands dominated by carnivorous reptiles and lush vegetation. We are captivated by the unusual, the mysterious: carnivorous pitcher plants, sundews and floating bladderworts of the Okefenokee bogs; parrot feathers, green-fly orchids, floating mosquito ferns and giant buttressed cypress of Ebenezer Creek's backwaters.

Ebenezer Creek, Georgia's only coastal stream designated a Wild and Scenic River, is a backwater stream. It is an elongated lake with slow drainage through sediments accumulated at its mouth causing the water to back up, hence a "backwater stream." Long periods of inundation may be responsible for the greatly enlarged bases of its cypress and tupelo. Not large in diameter for their old age, some reach 100 feet into the air. The creek's intimate passageways, striking high bluffs, abundant wildlife and primordial aspect are enchantments that entice us there.

Alligator in midday sun, Okefenokee Swamp

Giant buttressed bald cypress with a fringe of parrot feather, Ebenezer Creek

The rust-bronze color of pine needles compliments new-growth bracken ferns — a typical sight after a Coastal Plain forest burn. Notable are the golden blades of dried palmetto fronds and charred fire rings on the pines, a sure sign of recent fire, probably a control burn. Control burning is the technique of intentionally setting fires to eliminate the buildup of ground litter that makes good tinder, thus preventing natural fires from burning out of control.

One of the first plants to appear after a burn, bracken ferns are strong and coarse, often growing in large colonies with knee-high, almost horizontal wavy leaves. Most ferns grow in rich, moist, limy soil. In contrast, bracken ferns are usually indicators of poor and barren soil, such as this burned-over sandy area.

Bracken ferns and palmettos recover from a pine forest burn, Crooked River State Park

An emerald swath of high marsh on the mainland edge of Georgia's tidal marshlands is the interface between salt water and fresh, between mainland and Barrier Islands, systems that tolerate — and are driven by — alternating fresh- and saltwater inundation.

The silvery sea myrtle is situated above high tide while the black needlerush is located on moderately high ground where it is flooded only by storm and spring tides. The pale green cordgrass thrives in the lower marsh with twice-daily tidal flooding.

This is the edge zone, the marginal area between land and sea, similar to that described by poet Sidney Lanier in "The Marshes of Glynn": "Bending your beauty aside, with a step I stand / On the firm-packed sand, / Free / By a world of marsh that borders a world of sea. / Sinuous southward and sinuous northward the shimmering / band / Of the sand-beach fastens the fringe of the marsh to the / folds of the land. . . .a league of marsh-grass, waist-high, broad in / the blade, / Green, and all of a height, and unflecked with a light or a / shade, / Stretch leisurely off, in a pleasant plain, / To the terminal blue of the main. / Oh, what is abroad in the marsh and the terminal sea? / Somehow my soul seems suddenly free / From the weighing of fate and the sad discussion of sin, / By the length and the breadth and the sweep of the marshes / of Glynn."

Sea myrtle with black needlerush and cordgrass, Shellman Bluff area

BARRIER ISLANDS AND ESTUARIES

Richard G. Wiegert

On satellite photos the Barrier Islands can be compared to a string of jewels stretched along the Georgia coast from the mouth of the Savannah River in the north to the Saint Marys River in the south. In truth, some of the most precious landscapes of Georgia are found on these islands and their associated tidal marshes. Not only are these ecosystems aesthetically beautiful, but they are valuable as well, for both recreation and as nurseries for the coastal commercial fisheries.

Geologically, the entire Lower Coastal Plain of Georgia comprises a series of terraces resulting from the emergence of Barrier Islands, the sedimentary filling of the marshes behind them, and the formation of a new string of islands as the land continued its slow rise. Each of the terraces and sand ridges was formed during the fall and rise of sea level during a glacial period. All include the present major islands, formed during the Pleistocene epoch beginning about 2 million years ago. A few smaller islands, such as Blackbeard and Little Saint Simons, date from the most recent glaciation about 10,000 years ago, during the Holocene epoch. These latter islands will eventually become the major barrier islands of the next glacial period.

The major islands have a seaward beach zone with a broad sloping beach backed by protective dunes partially stabilized by clumps of attractive sea oats, a grass now protected because of its overexploitation for floral arrangements. Behind the dunes the islands comprise a mixture of low freshwater wetlands and broad "hammocks" or islands of elevation sufficient to permit the survival of ancient live oaks covered with Spanish moss. Much of the present island terrestrial environment is the result of clearing and draining as well as diking for rice culture that began in the late 1700s and continued on some islands until the early part of this century. Agricultural operations have been suspended on most of the land for many decades, and large areas are now covered in pine forest.

Landward of the islands, protected from oceanic waves, the shallow parts of the estuaries form tidal salt marsh. Along the land margins and in some brackish or very high salinity areas there are a number of grasses, rushes and other vascular plants. But vast expanses of this intertidal area are dominated by smooth cordgrass, *Spartina alteriflora*. Because of the physical

domination of cordgrass, it is easy to imagine that it is the only plant of importance.

Yet on the mud's surface in the marsh and on the tidal creek banks, hundreds of species of algae contribute more than 10 percent of the plant food used in the marsh ecosystem. Most of these consumers are microbes or tiny invertebrates. These form the base of food chains extending upward to the animals of direct interest to humans and may use the marsh proper only during its submergence at high tide. Twice each day the tidal marshes of Georgia are submerged, allowing strictly aquatic animals to forage for food. In between tides, when the surface of the marsh is exposed, birds, mammals and resident invertebrates such as fiddler crabs also feed from the marsh.

The beauty and recreational value of the Barrier Islands and estuaries inevitably create problems. The major difficulty is their inaccessibility. Any proposal for increased development of the islands and their surrounding marshes ultimately calls for causeways, bridges and marinas, which can quickly change the tidal flow patterns to the detriment of the marshes. This can adversely affect the nursery function of the marsh for juvenile shrimp, the growth of commercial blue crab populations and the recreational fishing provided by tidal creeks. Fortunately, the majority of the Barrier Islands of Georgia are not connected to the mainland by bridges and most currently enjoy some form of protective ownership such by the state, federal government or private foundations or organizations. This should guarantee freedom from deleterious development in the future and at the same time provide for non-destructive enjoyment by the public of this precious heritage.

Dr. Richard G. Wiegert is professor of zoology at the University of Georgia, an expert on salt marshes and a master modeler. When not conducting field studies, he is usually at his computer developing ecological models. Recently he has worked on modeling the ecology of hot springs in Yellowstone National Park, the ecology of blue crabs at Sapelo Island and the effects of water movement on spartina growth. His ecological modeling helped prove Eugene Odum's important theory of productivity and value of the salt marsh.

Above: Sunrise on incoming tide at boneyard, Wassaw Island
Opposite: Cockle shells and blue crab claw with sand dollars, Wassaw Island Beach

Reproductive stalks of cinnamon fern, Saint Simons Island

Morning dew on wolf spider webs, Cumberland Island
Overleaf: Shorebird tracks on shifting dunes, Cumberland Island

Dune swale grasses, Ossabaw Island

Island maritime forests must withstand the forces of time, and here on the banks of the Brickhill River, a stalwart pine is put to the test. A natural process is occurring: even though this tidal riverbank is eroding, the saltmarsh cordgrasses are already beginning to recover the shallows and collect sediments that will again restabilize the area.

On these landward banks, great piles of discarded oyster shells can be found, left by the Timucuans, a prehistoric Native American tribe that found Cumberland bluffs ideal for their flourishing villages. A special dark-gray marsh clay for making bricks was gathered by European settlers here. When fired, the clay turns a beautiful red color, hence the name *Brickhill Bluff*.

On the seaward side of Ossabaw Island (left) is a wet, undulating grassy meadow — a dune swale — banked by a young maritime forest of slash pines and small live oaks that emerged where plantation owners once grew cotton and indigo.

Slash pine at Brickhill Bluff above the Brickhill River, Cumberland Island

New life arises out of decaying matter on this mossy live oak, displaying repetitive patterns and orange-colored fungi. The moist moss-covered tree bark with various interdependent species is a mini-ecosystem.

In contrast with the miniature moss-lichen community on the live oak, the offshore ocean floor sustains a massive habitat of bottom-dwelling life. As the rhythmic tides deposit abundant living and dead treasures on shore (right), beachcombers are the fortunate recipients. Evidenced by the tiny holes near the shells' valves, many bivalves have fallen victim to the predacious oyster drill, a small mollusk. Over hundreds of years, shells like these — once homes for living animals — are broken and crushed by the sea, ground into the sand that forms these beaches.

Bracket fungi with lichen- and moss-covered live oak, Saint Catherine's Island

Shells and leopard crab at low tide, Cumberland Island

Battered and beaten, weathered and worn, live oaks can be elegantly sculpted friends and guardians in a storm. A story is told of a man climbing and tying himself to a sturdy live oak, relying on the tree's strength and resilience, and surviving a momentous storm. These characteristics, as well as their graceful curvature, also made the live oak valuable for wooden ship building. Many of the larger, older trees were cut.

The low, year-round live oak canopy filters the bright sunlight, painting a Renoirlike image of dappled light on the canvas of the open forest floor (above). Often called an evergreen because it is never seen without leaves, the live oak is deciduous. Once a year, near the end of March, the leaves drop to the ground continuously — sounding like rain — as new leaflets pop out nearly all at once, pushing off last year's growth and making a new spring "evergreen" tree.

Saw palmettos skirt the trunks of ancient live oaks, Cumberland Island

Sunrise on sabal palms and dead oaks, Wassaw Island

Early light on eroded bluffs of North Beach, Saint Catherines Island

Dog fennel, saw palmetto and dune grasses at Flag Pond, Wassaw Island

Longleaf pine at the edge of a sea of black needlerush and cordgrass, Ossabaw Island

In a sunny interdune meadow grow handsome native yuccas, beach croton and salt meadow hay. Rabbits and rattlesnakes forage here; feral pigs root and deer graze on the hay. Some of the islands house feral horses and cows. Though picturesque, the hoofed animals heavily impact island ecology by overgrazing and wearing down dunes.

Preservation is the watchword, and separation from the mainland by miles of salt marsh (left) has contributed to the preservation of many of Georgia's Barrier Islands from 20th century development. Most were rather inaccessible and generally ignored after being abandoned by the great plantation owners during the Civil War. Wealthy industrialists purchased many of the islands nearly intact in the late 1800s to early 1900s for retreats and hunting — deer, wild boar, wild turkey, alligator and bear were all fair game. Enlightened modern owners — many, descendants of turn-of-the-century purchasers — have found ways to maintain the islands' natural heritage while sharing the unique environment with others.

Native yucca in interdune meadow, Ossabaw Island

Afternoon sun casts long shadows over encroaching north-end sands below sabal palms. Although Wassaw Island is Georgia's most natural and least-changed island by human hands, it is nevertheless ever-changing at the hands of nature. As evidenced here by the shifting dunes and dead live oaks midbeach, the island is eroding away at the north end but building up on the south end, slowly moving southward. Pristine in its beauty, Wassaw claims several endangered species: bald eagle, peregrine falcon, nesting loggerhead turtle, diamondback terrapin and shortnose sturgeon of Wassaw Sound.

The quiet current of low tide in Sapelo's salt marsh appears peaceful (right), but the downed, dead trees along the bank indicate that a great volume of water enters and leaves the creek twice daily. The tidal mudbanks contain numerous marine invertebrates — mussels, clams, oysters, fiddler crabs — and provide an ideal feeding ground for wading birds and raccoons.

Sabal palms and shifting sands, Wassaw Island

Morning at tidal Barn Creek, Sapelo Island
Overleaf: Sunset reflected in tide runnel at South End Beach, Ossabaw Island

Cordgrass covered by shifting dunes along the north shore, Little Tybee Island

Georgia's tidal marshes and estuaries are described as some of the most naturally fertile landscapes in the world. There are few places that provide such good protection and so many nutrients for the growth and development of so many species. Overlooking the expanse of salt marsh on the south end of Sapelo, one can only imagine the amount of productivity hidden in the marsh depths. Georgia's tides are the highest in the Southeast, with seven-foot normal daily tides and nine-foot spring tides.

An oceanside marsh on Little Tybee is being covered over by moving dunes (left). Looking closely, one can see exquisite little salt crystals on the green cordgrass leaves in the foreground. Adapted to a salty environment, cordgrass leaves have glands that excrete excess salt. The beaches of Little Tybee also provide nesting grounds for the endangered loggerhead turtle and the pipping plover.

Needlerush and cordgrass around distant isolated hammock in south end salt marsh, Sapelo Island

Ancient live oak remains, Saint Catherines Island

For lovers of the Barrier Islands, it is difficult to imagine a more peaceful or rejuvenating scene than sunset over a tidal creek. Little Saint Simons Island and the Mosquito River skirting it are a nature lover's paradise with old forests and ancient sand dunes, wide beaches and young sand dunes, freshwater ponds and brackish water ponds, salt marsh and tidal creeks. The island is entirely owned by one family and used as a nature park. Bird-watching is preeminent, but alligators and other wildlife abound.

Saint Catherines Island (left) is also privately owned. A small segment is home to the Bronx Zoo's Wildlife Survival Center and is used to breed rare and endangered species from around the world for preservation. As with all of Georgia's Barrier Islands, Saint Catherines is slowly moving southward due to erosion from the prevailing winds and currents. As the island erodes, dead trees become haunting monuments to themselves in *boneyards*, as they are called.

Sunset over tidal waters of Mosquito River, Little Saint Simons Island

White sands blow across a wet beach at low tide to provide a subtle palette of textured grays. In contrast, a community of lichens and ferns living in balance on a live oak present a colorful image. Unfurling in verdant splendor when wet, the resurrection fern appears dead when it curls in a tight rust-brown ball during dry weather.

Blackbeard Island National Wildlife Refuge is the ideal place to experience the subtleties of nature: to walk a beach, to hike a trail through old-growth forest or marshland, to explore the many ponds that provide sanctuary for migratory fowl and alligators.

In closeup, as in landscape, colors, textures and patterns can inspire concern about the care of the earth's natural environments. We are reminded that people are not the world's only artists or architects. We do not need to understand our natural environment to enjoy it, but we do need understanding to preserve it. May we be a participant in the balance of nature, not a destroyer.

Calico crab shell, Blackbeard Island

Resurrection fern, lichens and mosses cling to live oak tree, Ossabaw Island

Technical Information

The majority of the images within this book were made with a Wista 45 SP field view camera, using lenses of 75mm, 90mm, 135mm, 210mm, 300mm and 400mm focal lengths. Additional work was taken with a Pentax 6x7 singles lens reflex camera using lenses from 45mm to 135mm. Fuji films were exclusively used to make the original transparencies. Filters used were a graduated warming filter, 81A, and a polarizing filter to cut down on glare when needed.

Exposures were calculated with a Minolta Auto Meter and a Pentax digital 1-degree spot meter by using reflected light from 30 seconds to 1/60 of a second. Apertures varied from f/11 to f/64. The transparencies were separated by the printer on state-of-the-art laser-scanning equipment. In every case an attempt was made to match the printed page with the original transparency.

Dense interior forest of mature pines, live oaks, palms and saw palmettos, Wassaw Island

GEORGIA

N

Tennessee

North Carolina

VALLEY AND PLATEAU

Chatahoochee National Forest

Brasstown Bald

APPALACHIAN MOUNTAINS

Carters Lake

Rome

Lake Sidney Lanier

Hartwell Lake

Alatoonah Lake

Athens

Atlanta

Chatahoochee River

Clarks Hill Lake

PIEDMONT

West Point Lake

Lake Sinclair

Augusta

Savannah River

Columbus

Macon

UPPER COASTAL PLAIN

South Carolina

Oconee River

Ocmulgee River

Ogeechee River

Savannah

Chattahoochee River

Albany

Altamaha River

Flint River

LOWER COASTAL PLAIN

Spring River

Satilla River

BARRIER ISLANDS AND ESTUARIES

Lake Seminole

Valdosta

Okefenokee

Florida

Swamp

Atlantic Ocean